A
grATTITUDE
journal
to
help
you
end
the
day
on
top.

Own
the
day
with
this
daily,
guided,
fill-in
journal!

Gratitude
w/
attitude

A
positive
&
motivational
gratitude
journal
based
on
the
swear
word
bitch?

Yes.

It's
called
a
bitch
win.

Date: ___ / ___ / ___

Day of the Week

S M T W TH F S

AM
PM

Bitch, You're the Best!

(Name of person, pet, or thing)

My Most Bitchin' Moment

_____

_____

_____

_____

_____

THE NUMBER OF FUCKS I DON'T GIVE TODAY

I'm fucking thankful for:

Pearls of *Wisdom*

Bitch-errific Ramblings!

_____

_____

_____

_____

_____

_____

_____

Shit to do

☐ _____

☐ _____

☐ _____

☐ _____

☐ _____

☐ _____

☐ _____

☐ _____

"**Boss Bitch**"
is my
co-pilot and
"**I don't give
a shit**" is
what I'm
flying.

This or that: *Orange or grape soda? Heart or soul? Running or walking? Popcorn or peanuts? Bottle or glass? Charisma or luck? Giraffe or zebra?*

Date: ___/___/___

My Baddest Bitch!

(Name of person, pet, or thing)

Today's Bitchin' Experience

_____

_____

_____

_____

_____

THE NUMBER OF FUCKS I DON'T GIVE TODAY

I'm fucking thankful for:

Today's Playlist

My Bitch-mazing Thoughts!

_____

_____

_____

_____

_____

_____

_____

Shit to do

☐ _____

☐ _____

☐ _____

☐ _____

☐ _____

☐ _____

☐ _____

☐ _____

Random Crappery
Things I can improve...

This or that: Independent or team? Pierced or clip-on? Love or money? Digital or analog? Hot cocoa or coffee? sofa or couch? Flowers or trees?

Date: ___ / ___ / ___

Day of the Week
S M T W TH F S

AM
PM

Today's Bitchin' Bestie!

(Name of person, pet, or thing)

Bitch Win of the Day

_____
_____
_____
_____
_____

THE NUMBER OF FUCKS I DON'T GIVE TODAY

I'm fucking thankful for:

Create a *Masterpiece*

(or just scribble)

Bitch-sational Ramblings!

_____

_____

_____

_____

_____

_____

_____

Shit to do

- ☐ _____
- ☐ _____
- ☐ _____
- ☐ _____
- ☐ _____
- ☐ _____
- ☐ _____
- ☐ _____

Random Crappery
Word of the day...

THOUGHT OF THE DAY:

This or that: Yes or no? White or wheat bread? Big or small crowd? Soda or juice? Alaska or Hawaii? Shark or whale? Body wash or hand soap?

Date: ___/___/___

Day of the Week

S M T W TH F S

AM
PM

My Bitch in Crime!

(Name of person, pet, or thing)

Bitchin' Thing That Happened

_____

_____

_____

_____

_____

THE NUMBER OF FUCKS I DON'T GIVE TODAY

I'm fucking thankful for:

OMG-ossip!

More Bitch-tacular Writings!

_____

_____

_____

_____

_____

_____

_____

Shit to do

- ☐ _____
- ☐ _____
- ☐ _____
- ☐ _____
- ☐ _____
- ☐ _____
- ☐ _____
- ☐ _____

Random Crappery

These [＿＿＿＿] make me [＿＿＿＿].

This or that: Chat or gossip? Walk a dog or rock a baby? Arctic or tropical? Riches or Happiness? Comedy or Horror? Buffalo wings or potstickers?

Date: ___ / ___ / ___

Day of the Week

S M T W TH F S

AM

PM

This Bitch Made My Day!

(Name of person, pet, or thing)

Today's Bitchin' Highlight

_____

_____

_____

_____

THE NUMBER OF FUCKS I DON'T GIVE TODAY

I'm fucking thankful for:

Shopping
Wish List:

Other Bitch-tastic Happenings!

Shit to do

- [ ]
- [ ]
- [ ]
- [ ]
- [ ]
- [ ]
- [ ]
- [ ]

Random Crappery
Color of the day...

" QUOTE OF THE DAY: "

This or that: Kids or pets? Shy or fearless? Brush or comb? Zoo or aquarium? Candy or cake? Cookies or ice cream? Snowboarding or surfing?

Date: ___/___/___

Bitch, You're the Best!

(Name of person, pet, or thing)

My Most Bitchin' Moment

_____

_____

_____

_____

_____

THE NUMBER OF FUCKS I DON'T GIVE TODAY

I'm fucking thankful for:

Pearls of Wisdom

Bitch-errific Ramblings!

_____
_____
_____
_____
_____
_____
_____

Shit to do

☐ _____
☐ _____
☐ _____
☐ _____
☐ _____
☐ _____
☐ _____
☐ _____

"Impossible is nothing but a fucking opinion that doesn't matter."

This or that: Weird or normal? Thunderstorms or sunshine? Drive or fly? Snowball or water balloon? Theme park or water park? Sleep or play?

Date: ___/___/___

My Baddest Bitch!

(Name of person, pet, or thing)

Today's Bitchin' Experience

_____

_____

_____

_____

_____

THE NUMBER OF FUCKS I DON'T GIVE TODAY

I'm fucking thankful for:

Today's Playlist

My Bitch-mazing Thoughts!

_____

_____

_____

_____

_____

_____

_____

Shit to do

- [ ] _____
- [ ] _____
- [ ] _____
- [ ] _____
- [ ] _____
- [ ] _____
- [ ] _____
- [ ] _____

Random Crappery
Things I can improve...

This or that: Formal or casual? Purple or green? Handsome or smart? Protein or carb? Leader or follower? Reading or writing? Witches or wizards?

Date: ____ / ____ / ____

Day of the Week
S M T W TH F S

AM
PM

Today's Bitchin' Bestie!

(Name of person, pet, or thing)

Bitch Win of the Day

_____
_____
_____
_____
_____

THE NUMBER OF FUCKS I DON'T GIVE TODAY

I'm fucking thankful for:

Create a *Masterpiece*

(or just scribble)

Bitch-sational Ramblings!

_____
_____
_____
_____
_____
_____
_____

Shit to do

- ☐ _____
- ☐ _____
- ☐ _____
- ☐ _____
- ☐ _____
- ☐ _____
- ☐ _____
- ☐ _____

Random Crappery
Word of the day...

THOUGHT OF THE DAY:

This or that: Cat or dog? Swimming or sun bathing? Sculpture or painting? City or suburbs? Chocolate or vanilla? Long sleeve or short sleeve?

Date: _____ / / _____

My Bitch in Crime!

(Name of person, pet, or thing)

Bitchin' Thing That Happened

_____

_____

_____

_____

_____

THE NUMBER OF FUCKS I DON'T GIVE TODAY

I'm fucking thankful for:

OMG-ossip!

More Bitch-tacular Writings!

_____
_____
_____
_____
_____
_____
_____

Shit to do

- ☐ _____
- ☐ _____
- ☐ _____
- ☐ _____
- ☐ _____
- ☐ _____
- ☐ _____
- ☐ _____

Random Crappery

These [   ] make me [   ] .

This or that: Sun hats or sunglasses? Stop or go? Jeans or shorts? Logical or creative? Pink or blue? Santa or Easter bunny? Ice cream or popsicle?

Date: ___ / ___ / ___

Day of the Week
S M T W TH F S

AM
PM

This Bitch Made My Day!

(Name of person, pet, or thing)

Today's Bitchin' Highlight

_____
_____
_____
_____

THE NUMBER OF FUCKS I DON'T GIVE TODAY

I'm fucking thankful for:

Shopping
Wish List:

Other Bitch-tastic Happenings!

_____
_____
_____
_____
_____
_____
_____

Shit to do

☐ _____
☐ _____
☐ _____
☐ _____
☐ _____
☐ _____
☐ _____
☐ _____

Random Crappery
Color of the day...

" QUOTE OF THE DAY:

This or that: Newspapers or magazines? Lost or found? Hot coffee or iced coffee? Car or motorcycle? Medium rare or well done steak? Hands or feet?

Date: ___/___/___

Day of the Week
S M T W TH F S

AM
PM

Bitch, You're the Best!

(Name of person, pet, or thing)

My Most Bitchin' Moment

_____

_____

_____

_____

_____

THE NUMBER OF FUCKS I DON'T GIVE TODAY

🖕 🖕 🖕 🖕 🖕 🖕 🖕 🖕 🖕 🖕

I'm fucking thankful for:

Pearls of Wisdom

Bitch-errific Ramblings!

_____

_____

_____

_____

_____

_____

_____

Shit to do

- ☐ _____
- ☐ _____
- ☐ _____
- ☐ _____
- ☐ _____
- ☐ _____
- ☐ _____
- ☐ _____

> "Refuse mediocrity unless it's a fucking Monday. Then, refuse it even more!"

This or that: Hats or headbands? Trash or treasure? Adventurous or cautious? Past or future? Desktop or laptop? Hair or hat? Taste or smell?

Date: ___ / ___ / ___

Day of the Week

S M T W TH F S

AM
PM

My Baddest Bitch!

(Name of person, pet, or thing)

Today's Bitchin' Experience

_____

_____

_____

_____

_____

THE NUMBER OF FUCKS I DON'T GIVE TODAY

I'm fucking thankful for:

Today's Playlist

My Bitch-mazing Thoughts!

_____

_____

_____

_____

_____

_____

_____

Shit to do

☐ _____
☐ _____
☐ _____
☐ _____
☐ _____
☐ _____
☐ _____
☐ _____

Random Crappery
Things I can improve...

This or that: White or brown rice? Music or podcast? Beach or park? Boots or sandals? Dyed or natural hair? Golf or putt-putt? Raisins or nuts?

Date: ___ / ___ / ___

Today's Bitchin' Bestie!

(Name of person, pet, or thing)

Bitch Win of the Day

_____

_____

_____

_____

THE NUMBER OF FUCKS I DON'T GIVE TODAY

I'm fucking thankful for:

Create a
Masterpiece

(or just scribble)

Bitch-sational Ramblings!

_____
_____
_____
_____
_____
_____
_____

Shit to do

☐ _____
☐ _____
☐ _____
☐ _____
☐ _____
☐ _____
☐ _____
☐ _____

Random Crappery
Word of the day...

THOUGHT OF THE DAY:

This or that: T-shirt or tanktop? Concert or museum? Deer or elk?
Outgoing or shy? Casual or Dress? Chicken or beef? Cake or pie? Home or hotel?

Day of the Week
Date: _____ / / _____

S M T W TH F S

AM
PM

My Bitch in Crime!

(Name of person, pet, or thing)

Bitchin' Thing That Happened

_____
_____
_____
_____

THE NUMBER OF FUCKS I DON'T GIVE TODAY

I'm fucking thankful for:

OMG-ossip!

More Bitch-tacular Writings!

_____

_____

_____

_____

_____

_____

_____

Shit to do

- ☐ _____
- ☐ _____
- ☐ _____
- ☐ _____
- ☐ _____
- ☐ _____
- ☐ _____
- ☐ _____

Random Crappery

These [＿＿＿＿] make me [＿＿＿＿] .

This or that: _Pandas or whales? Talking or listening? Rain or shine? Video games or computer games? Sunburn or mosquito bite? Pink or Turquoise?_

Date: ___ / ___ / ___

Day of the Week

S M T W TH F S

AM
PM

This Bitch Made My Day!

(Name of person, pet, or thing)

Today's Bitchin' Highlight

_____
_____
_____
_____
_____

THE NUMBER OF FUCKS I DON'T GIVE TODAY

I'm fucking thankful for:

Shopping
Wish List:

Other Bitch-tastic Happenings!

_____

_____

_____

_____

_____

_____

_____

Shit to do

- ☐ _____
- ☐ _____
- ☐ _____
- ☐ _____
- ☐ _____
- ☐ _____
- ☐ _____
- ☐ _____

Random Crappery
Color of the day...

QUOTE OF THE DAY:

This or that: Neutral tones or bold colors? Laptop or phone? Mansion or cabin? Day or night? Bonfire or fireplace? Sports or reading? Sweet or savory?

Date: ___/___/___

Bitch, You're the Best!

(Name of person, pet, or thing)

My Most Bitchin' Moment

_____
_____
_____
_____
_____

THE NUMBER OF FUCKS I DON'T GIVE TODAY

I'm fucking thankful for:

Pearls of Wisdom

Bitch-errific Ramblings!

_____
_____
_____
_____
_____
_____
_____

Shit to do

- [ ] _____
- [ ] _____
- [ ] _____
- [ ] _____
- [ ] _____
- [ ] _____
- [ ] _____
- [ ] _____

> Time machines don't exist. Forget traveling to the past & move the fuck on!

This or that: Sweater or Hoodies? Sugar or spice? Breakfast or dinner? Roses or daisies? Pudding or custard? Smart or beautiful? Red or blue?

Date: ___ / ___ / ___

Day of the Week

S M T W TH F S

AM
PM

My Baddest Bitch!

(Name of person, pet, or thing)

Today's Bitchin' Experience

_____

_____

_____

_____

_____

THE NUMBER OF FUCKS I DON'T GIVE TODAY

I'm fucking thankful for:

Today's Playlist

My Bitch-mazing Thoughts!

_____
_____
_____
_____
_____
_____
_____

Shit to do

- ☐ _____
- ☐ _____
- ☐ _____
- ☐ _____
- ☐ _____
- ☐ _____
- ☐ _____
- ☐ _____

Random Crappery
Things I can improve...

This or that: Hugs or Kisses? Nice car or nice house? Biscuits or toast? Camping or hiking? Soup or sandwich? Soup or salad? Dragon or unicorn?

Date: ___ / ___ / ___

Day of the Week
S M T W TH F S

AM
PM

Today's Bitchin' Bestie!

(Name of person, pet, or thing)

Bitch Win of the Day

_____
_____
_____
_____
_____

THE NUMBER OF FUCKS I DON'T GIVE TODAY

I'm fucking thankful for:

Create a Masterpiece

(or just scribble)

Bitch-sational Ramblings!

Shit to do

- ☐ _____
- ☐ _____
- ☐ _____
- ☐ _____
- ☐ _____
- ☐ _____
- ☐ _____
- ☐ _____

Random Crappery
Word of the day...

THOUGHT OF THE DAY:

This or that: _Still or sparkling? Fly or teleportation? Mars or earth? Online or offline shopping? Summer or winter? Subway or car? City or farm? One or Two?_

Date: _____ / / _____

My Bitch in Crime!

(Name of person, pet, or thing)

Bitchin' Thing That Happened

_____
_____
_____
_____
_____

THE NUMBER OF FUCKS I DON'T GIVE TODAY

I'm fucking thankful for:

O.M.G-ossip!

More Bitch-tacular Writings!

_____
_____
_____
_____
_____
_____
_____

Shit to do

- ☐ _____
- ☐ _____
- ☐ _____
- ☐ _____
- ☐ _____
- ☐ _____
- ☐ _____
- ☐ _____

Random Crappery

These _____ make me _____ .

This or that: Strong or smart? Letter or postcard? Apples or bananas? Dark chocolate or white chocolate? Long or short hair? Vampire or wolf?

Date: _____ / ___ / ___

Day of the Week

S M T W TH F S

AM

PM

This Bitch Made My Day!

////////////////////

(Name of person, pet, or thing)

Today's Bitchin' Highlight

_____

_____

_____

_____

_____

THE NUMBER OF FUCKS I DON'T GIVE TODAY

I'm fucking thankful for:

Shopping
Wish List:

Other Bitch-tastic Happenings!

_____
_____
_____
_____
_____
_____
_____
_____
_____

Shit to do

☐ _____
☐ _____
☐ _____
☐ _____
☐ _____
☐ _____
☐ _____
☐ _____

Random Crappery
Color of the day...

" QUOTE OF THE DAY:

"

This or that: Selfie or group photo? Cupcake or Muffin? Staple or paper clip? New York or London? Smoothie or milkshake? Sunrise or sunset?

Date: ___ / ___ / ___

Day of the Week

S M T W TH F S

AM

PM

Bitch, You're the Best!

(Name of person, pet, or thing)

My Most Bitchin' Moment

_____

_____

_____

_____

_____

THE NUMBER OF FUCKS I DON'T GIVE TODAY

I'm fucking thankful for:

Pearls of Wisdom

Bitch-errific Ramblings!

Shit to do

- [ ] _____
- [ ] _____
- [ ] _____
- [ ] _____
- [ ] _____
- [ ] _____
- [ ] _____
- [ ] _____

" If you get fucking tired of being knocked down, then do the knocking! "

This or that: Jacket or sweater? Bacon or sausage? Earthquake or tornado? Drive or walk? Basket or box? Headphones or earbuds? Gold or silver?

Date: ___/___/___

My Baddest Bitch!

(Name of person, pet, or thing)

Today's Bitchin' Experience

_____

_____

_____

_____

_____

THE NUMBER OF FUCKS I DON'T GIVE TODAY

I'm fucking thankful for:

Today's Playlist

My Bitch-mazing Thoughts!

_____
_____
_____
_____
_____
_____
_____

Shit to do

- ☐ _____
- ☐ _____
- ☐ _____
- ☐ _____
- ☐ _____
- ☐ _____
- ☐ _____
- ☐ _____

Random Crappery
Things I can improve...

This or that: Western or Sci Fi? Wedding or birthday? Sweet or sour? Chips or trail mix? Glasses or contacts? Rain or wind? Spend or save? Text or chat?

Date: ___ / ___ / ___

Day of the Week

S M T W TH F S

AM
PM

Today's Bitchin' Bestie!

(Name of person, pet, or thing)

Bitch Win of the Day

_____
_____
_____
_____
_____

THE NUMBER OF FUCKS I DON'T GIVE TODAY

I'm fucking thankful for:

Create a Masterpiece

(or just scribble)

Bitch-sational Ramblings!

_____
_____
_____
_____
_____
_____
_____
_____

Shit to do

- ☐ _____
- ☐ _____
- ☐ _____
- ☐ _____
- ☐ _____
- ☐ _____
- ☐ _____
- ☐ _____

Random Crappery
Word of the day...

THOUGHT OF THE DAY:

This or that: Heater or fan? Meat or vegetables? Skateboard or bicycle? Skiing or snowboarding? Bowling or golf? Boat or plane? Bacon or eggs?

Date: _____ / / _____

My Bitch in Crime!

(Name of person, pet, or thing)

Bitchin' Thing That Happened

_____
_____
_____
_____
_____

THE NUMBER OF FUCKS I DON'T GIVE TODAY

I'm fucking thankful for:

OMG-ossip!

More Bitch-tacular Writings!

_____
_____
_____
_____
_____
_____
_____
_____

Shit to do

- ☐ _____
- ☐ _____
- ☐ _____
- ☐ _____
- ☐ _____
- ☐ _____
- ☐ _____
- ☐ _____

Random Crappery

These [   ] make me [   ] .

This or that: Lemonade or ice tea? Meat or cheese? Library or cafe? Left or right handed? Laundry or dishes? Perfume or body spray? Close or far?

Date: ___ / ___ / ___

Day of the Week

S M T W TH F S

AM

PM

This Bitch Made My Day!

(Name of person, pet, or thing)

Today's Bitchin' Highlight

_____

_____

_____

_____

_____

THE NUMBER OF FUCKS I DON'T GIVE TODAY

I'm fucking thankful for:

Shopping Wish List:

Other Bitch-tastic Happenings!

_____
_____
_____
_____
_____
_____
_____

Shit to do

Random Crappery
Color of the day...

- ☐ _____
- ☐ _____
- ☐ _____
- ☐ _____
- ☐ _____
- ☐ _____
- ☐ _____
- ☐ _____

❝
QUOTE OF THE DAY:
❞

This or that: Frozen pizza or delivery? Silver or gold? Dinosaurs or sea monsters? Cleaning house or doing dishes? Matches or lighters?

Date: ___/___/___

Day of the Week

S M T W TH F S

AM
PM

Bitch, You're the Best!

////////////////////////////

(Name of person, pet, or thing)

My Most Bitchin' Moment

_____

_____

_____

_____

_____

THE NUMBER OF FUCKS I DON'T GIVE TODAY

I'm fucking thankful for:

Pearls of Wisdom

Bitch-errific Ramblings!

_____
_____
_____
_____
_____
_____
_____

Shit to do

- [ ] _____
- [ ] _____
- [ ] _____
- [ ] _____
- [ ] _____
- [ ] _____
- [ ] _____
- [ ] _____

" You're never too old to be the baddest bitch on the planet! "

This or that: Guitar or piano? Jupiter or Saturn? Socks or barefoot? Air conditioner or ceiling fan? Shower or bubble bath? Apple or orange?

Date: ___ / ___ / ___

Day of the Week

S M T W TH F S

AM
PM

My Baddest Bitch!

(Name of person, pet, or thing)

Today's Bitchin' Experience

_____

_____

_____

_____

_____

THE NUMBER OF FUCKS I DON'T GIVE TODAY

I'm fucking thankful for:

Today's Playlist

My Bitch-mazing Thoughts!

_____
_____
_____
_____
_____
_____
_____

Shit to do

Random Crappery
Things I can improve...

☐ _____
☐ _____
☐ _____
☐ _____
☐ _____
☐ _____
☐ _____
☐ _____

This or that: Indoor or Outdoor? Friday or Saturday? Flannel or floral? Ferris wheel or roller coaster? Library or museum? Salt or pepper?

Date: ___ / ___ / ___

Day of the Week
S M T W TH F S

AM
PM

Today's Bitchin' Bestie!

(Name of person, pet, or thing)

Bitch Win of the Day

_____
_____
_____
_____
_____

THE NUMBER OF FUCKS I DON'T GIVE TODAY

I'm fucking thankful for:

Create a *Masterpiece*

(or just scribble)

Bitch-sational Ramblings!

_____
_____
_____
_____
_____
_____
_____
_____

Shit to do

☐ _____
☐ _____
☐ _____
☐ _____
☐ _____
☐ _____
☐ _____
☐ _____

Random Crappery
Word of the day...

THOUGHT OF THE DAY:

This or that: Touch or taste? Bunny or squirrel? Read minds or turn invisible? Punch or kick? Theater or cinema? Singing or listening to music?

My Bitch in Crime!

(Name of person, pet, or thing)

Bitchin' Thing That Happened

_____

_____

_____

_____

_____

THE NUMBER OF FUCKS I DON'T GIVE TODAY

I'm fucking thankful for:

OMG-ossip!

More Bitch-tacular Writings!

Shit to do

- [ ] _____
- [ ] _____
- [ ] _____
- [ ] _____
- [ ] _____
- [ ] _____
- [ ] _____
- [ ] _____

Random Crappery

These [_____] make me [_____].

This or that: Scrambled or over-easy eggs? Slacker or overachiever? Red or Pink? Hard or soft tacos? Gloves or mittens? Blanket or comforter?

Date: ___ / ___ / ___

Day of the Week

S M T W TH F S

AM

PM

This Bitch Made My Day!

(Name of person, pet, or thing)

Today's Bitchin' Highlight

_____

_____

_____

_____

_____

THE NUMBER OF FUCKS I DON'T GIVE TODAY

I'm fucking thankful for:

Shopping
Wish List:

Other Bitch-tastic Happenings!

_____
_____
_____
_____
_____
_____
_____

Shit to do

☐ _____
☐ _____
☐ _____
☐ _____
☐ _____
☐ _____
☐ _____
☐ _____

Random Crappery
Color of the day...

" QUOTE OF THE DAY:

"

This or that: Ketchup or mustard? Vacation or staycation? Black or red? Blinds or curtains? Zip-up or pullover hoodie? Fast or slow? Real or fake?

Date: ___ / ___ / ___

Day of the Week

S M T W TH F S

AM
PM

Bitch, You're the Best!

(Name of person, pet, or thing)

My Most Bitchin' Moment

_____
_____
_____
_____
_____

THE NUMBER OF FUCKS I DON'T GIVE TODAY

I'm fucking thankful for:

Pearls of *Wisdom*

Bitch-errific Ramblings!

_____
_____
_____
_____
_____
_____
_____

Shit to do

- [ ] _____
- [ ] _____
- [ ] _____
- [ ] _____
- [ ] _____
- [ ] _____
- [ ] _____
- [ ] _____

" Be the Boss Bitch that You are and make your own fuck-ing rules. "

This or that: Cloth or paper? Hash browns or french fries? Romance or action? Yellow or orange? Funny or romantic? Thunderstorm or snowstorm?

Date: ___ / ___ / ___

Day of the Week
S M T W TH F S

AM
PM

My Baddest Bitch!

(Name of person, pet, or thing)

Today's Bitchin' Experience

_____

_____

_____

_____

_____

THE NUMBER OF FUCKS I DON'T GIVE TODAY

I'm fucking thankful for:

Today's Playlist

My Bitch-mazing Thoughts!

_____
_____
_____
_____
_____
_____
_____
_____

Shit to do

Random Crappery
Things I can improve...

- [ ] _____
- [ ] _____
- [ ] _____
- [ ] _____
- [ ] _____
- [ ] _____
- [ ] _____
- [ ] _____

This or that: Cute or beautiful? Butterflies or caterpillars? Sunglasses or sun visor? Rain or snow? Brains or beauty? Radio or television? 99 or 100?

Date: ___ / ___ / ___

Day of the Week

S M T W TH F S

AM

PM

Today's Bitchin' Bestie!

(Name of person, pet, or thing)

Bitch Win of the Day

_____

_____

_____

_____

_____

THE NUMBER OF FUCKS I DON'T GIVE TODAY

I'm fucking thankful for:

Create a
Masterpiece

(or just scribble)

Bitch-sational Ramblings!

Shit to do

- [ ]
- [ ]
- [ ]
- [ ]
- [ ]
- [ ]
- [ ]
- [ ]

Random Crappery
Word of the day...

THOUGHT OF THE DAY:

This or that: Sour cream or salsa? Home cooking or takeout? Shoulder bag or wallet? Yoga pants or jeans? Typing or texting? Circus or carnival?

Date: _____ / _____ / _____

Day of the Week

S M T W TH F S

AM

PM

My Bitch in Crime!

(Name of person, pet, or thing)

Bitchin' Thing That Happened

_____

_____

_____

_____

THE NUMBER OF FUCKS I DON'T GIVE TODAY

I'm fucking thankful for:

OMG-ossip!

More Bitch-tacular Writings!

_____
_____
_____
_____
_____
_____
_____

Shit to do

- ☐ _____
- ☐ _____
- ☐ _____
- ☐ _____
- ☐ _____
- ☐ _____
- ☐ _____
- ☐ _____

Random Crappery

These [_____] make me [_____].

This or that: Ocean or lake? Circles or squares? Costume party or pool party? Diamonds or rubies? Hammer or nail? Lazy or active? Sun or shade?

Date: ___/___/___

This Bitch Made My Day!

(Name of person, pet, or thing)

Today's Bitchin' Highlight

_____

_____

_____

_____

_____

THE NUMBER OF FUCKS I DON'T GIVE TODAY

I'm fucking thankful for:

Shopping
Wish List:

Other Bitch-tastic Happenings!

_____
_____
_____
_____
_____
_____
_____

Shit to do

- ☐ _____
- ☐ _____
- ☐ _____
- ☐ _____
- ☐ _____
- ☐ _____
- ☐ _____
- ☐ _____

Random Crappery
Color of the day...

QUOTE OF THE DAY:

This or that: Leather or fabric? Peanut butter or jelly? Hot weather or cold weather? Chips or popcorn? Pancakes or waffles? Passenger or driver?

Date: ___/___/___

Bitch, You're the Best!

(Name of person, pet, or thing)

My Most Bitchin' Moment

_____

_____

_____

_____

_____

THE NUMBER OF FUCKS I DON'T GIVE TODAY

I'm fucking thankful for:

Pearls of Wisdom

Bitch-errific Ramblings!

_____

_____

_____

_____

_____

_____

_____

Shit to do

☐ _____

☐ _____

☐ _____

☐ _____

☐ _____

☐ _____

☐ _____

☐ _____

> " You got two choices in life: Be a "little bitch" or Be the "BOSS BITCH!" "

This or that: Ability to fly or turn invisible? Movie or play? Asking or answering? Potato chips or potato salad? Friend or lover? Late or early?

Date: _____ / _____ / _____

Day of the Week

S M T W TH F S

AM

PM

My Baddest Bitch!

(Name of person, pet, or thing)

Today's Bitchin' Experience

_____

_____

_____

_____

THE NUMBER OF FUCKS I DON'T GIVE TODAY

I'm fucking thankful for:

Today's Playlist

My Bitch-mazing Thoughts!

_____
_____
_____
_____
_____
_____
_____

Shit to do

Random Crappery
Things I can improve...

☐ _____
☐ _____
☐ _____
☐ _____
☐ _____
☐ _____
☐ _____
☐ _____

This or that: Healthy or comfort food? Gummy worm or gummy bear? Scarf or beanie? Party person or small gatherings? Saturday or Sunday?

Date: ___ / ___ / ___

Day of the Week
S M T W TH F S

AM
PM

Today's Bitchin' Bestie!

(Name of person, pet, or thing)

Bitch Win of the Day

_____

_____

_____

_____

_____

THE NUMBER OF FUCKS I DON'T GIVE TODAY

I'm fucking thankful for:

Create a _Masterpiece_

(or just scribble)

Bitch-sational Ramblings!

Shit to do

- [ ] _____
- [ ] _____
- [ ] _____
- [ ] _____
- [ ] _____
- [ ] _____
- [ ] _____
- [ ] _____

Random Crappery
Word of the day...

THOUGHT OF THE DAY:

This or that: Tent or RV? Fruit or vegetable? Watch or participate? Genius or wealthy? Art or science? Tattoo or piercings? Burgers or tacos?

Date: ___/___/___

Day of the Week
S M T W TH F S

AM
PM

My Bitch in Crime!

(Name of person, pet, or thing)

Bitchin' Thing That Happened

_____
_____
_____
_____
_____

THE NUMBER OF FUCKS I DON'T GIVE TODAY

I'm fucking thankful for:

OMG-ossip!

More Bitch-tacular Writings!

_____
_____
_____
_____
_____
_____
_____

Shit to do

☐ _____
☐ _____
☐ _____
☐ _____
☐ _____
☐ _____
☐ _____
☐ _____

Random Crappery

These [_____] make me [_____].

This or that: Sit-ups or push ups? Meat or fish? Ninja or samurai? City or country? Singing or dancing? Spring or summer? BBQ or restaurant?

Date: ___/___/___

This Bitch Made My Day!

(Name of person, pet, or thing)

Today's Bitchin' Highlight

_____

_____

_____

_____

THE NUMBER OF FUCKS I DON'T GIVE TODAY

I'm fucking thankful for:

Shopping Wish List:

Other Bitch-tastic Happenings!

_____
_____
_____
_____
_____
_____
_____

Shit to do

- ☐ _____
- ☐ _____
- ☐ _____
- ☐ _____
- ☐ _____
- ☐ _____
- ☐ _____
- ☐ _____

Random Crappery
Color of the day...

QUOTE OF THE DAY:

This or that: Carpet or hardwood floors? Frozen yogurt or ice cream? Sun or moon? Zombies or aliens? Rice or noodles? Paper or plastic? Work or play?

Date: ___/___/___

Day of the Week
S M T W TH F S

AM
PM

Bitch, You're the Best!

(Name of person, pet, or thing)

My Most Bitchin' Moment

_____

_____

_____

_____

_____

THE NUMBER OF FUCKS I DON'T GIVE TODAY

I'm fucking thankful for:

Pearls of Wisdom

Bitch-errific Ramblings!

_____
_____
_____
_____
_____
_____
_____

Shit to do

- ☐ _____
- ☐ _____
- ☐ _____
- ☐ _____
- ☐ _____
- ☐ _____
- ☐ _____
- ☐ _____

> "Everyday is a new day to get off your ass and conquer your goals."

This or that: Passive or defiant? Fast food or homemade? Pop music or rock music? Comedy or horror? Real plant or fake plant? White or Cream?

Date: ___/___/___

Day of the Week

S M T W TH F S

AM

PM

My Baddest Bitch!

(Name of person, pet, or thing)

Today's Bitchin' Experience

_____

_____

_____

_____

THE NUMBER OF FUCKS I DON'T GIVE TODAY

I'm fucking thankful for:

Today's Playlist

My Bitch-mazing Thoughts!

_____
_____
_____
_____
_____
_____
_____

Shit to do

- ☐ _____
- ☐ _____
- ☐ _____
- ☐ _____
- ☐ _____
- ☐ _____
- ☐ _____
- ☐ _____

Random Crappery
Things I can improve...

This or that: Wash dishes or mow lawn? Solo trip or family trip? Introvert or extrovert? Comedy or chic flick? Necklace or bracelet? Fall or winter?

Date: ___ / ___ / ___

Day of the Week

S M T W TH F S

AM
PM

Today's Bitchin' Bestie!

(Name of person, pet, or thing)

Bitch Win of the Day

_____

_____

_____

_____

THE NUMBER OF FUCKS I DON'T GIVE TODAY

I'm fucking thankful for:

Create a *Masterpiece*

(or just scribble)

Bitch-sational Ramblings!

_____

_____

_____

_____

_____

_____

_____

Shit to do

☐ _____

☐ _____

☐ _____

☐ _____

☐ _____

☐ _____

☐ _____

☐ _____

Random Crappery
Word of the day...

THOUGHT OF THE DAY:

This or that: Fame or friends? High school or college? Swimming or hiking? Beef jerky or pepperoni stick? Crossword or word search? Weights or treadmill?

Date: ___ / ___ / ___

My Bitch in Crime!

(Name of person, pet, or thing)

Bitchin' Thing That Happened

_____

_____

_____

_____

_____

THE NUMBER OF FUCKS I DON'T GIVE TODAY

I'm fucking thankful for:

OMG-ossip!

More Bitch-tacular Writings!

_____
_____
_____
_____
_____
_____
_____

Shit to do

☐ _____
☐ _____
☐ _____
☐ _____
☐ _____
☐ _____
☐ _____
☐ _____

Random Crappery

These [____] make me [____] .

This or that: Rocket or satelliite? Picnic or restaurant? Toothpaste or deodorant? Sneakers or boots? Sunblock or sunscreen? Superheroes or super villains?

Date: ___ / ___ / ___

Day of the Week
S M T W TH F S

AM
PM

This Bitch Made My Day!

(Name of person, pet, or thing)

Today's Bitchin' Highlight

_____

_____

_____

_____

_____

THE NUMBER OF FUCKS I DON'T GIVE TODAY

I'm fucking thankful for:

Shopping
Wish List:

Other Bitch-tastic Happenings!

_____
_____
_____
_____
_____
_____
_____

Shit to do

- ☐ _____
- ☐ _____
- ☐ _____
- ☐ _____
- ☐ _____
- ☐ _____
- ☐ _____
- ☐ _____

Random Crappery
Color of the day...

" QUOTE OF THE DAY:

This or that: _Email or letter? Beach or mountain? Fish or bird? Stop time or teleport? Straw hat or baseball cap? Comedy or drama? Give or receive?_

Date: ____/____/____

Day of the Week
S M T W TH F S

AM
PM

Bitch, You're the Best!

My Most Bitchin' Moment

_____

_____

_____

_____

_____

THE NUMBER OF FUCKS I DON'T GIVE TODAY

I'm fucking thankful for:

Pearls of Wisdom

Bitch-errific Ramblings!

Shit to do

- [ ]
- [ ]
- [ ]
- [ ]
- [ ]
- [ ]
- [ ]
- [ ]

> "If people are giving you shit, be the better bitch and take the high road."

This or that: Card games or board games? Shower or tub? Hot or mild sauce? Rock or hip hop? Rent or buy? Cruise ship or resort? Organized or messy?

Date: ___ / ___ / ___

My Baddest Bitch!

(Name of person, pet, or thing)

Today's Bitchin' Experience

_____

_____

_____

_____

_____

THE NUMBER OF FUCKS I DON'T GIVE TODAY

I'm fucking thankful for:

Today's Playlist

My Bitch-mazing Thoughts!

_____
_____
_____
_____
_____
_____
_____

Shit to do

Random Crappery
Things I can improve...

- [ ] _____
- [ ] _____
- [ ] _____
- [ ] _____
- [ ] _____
- [ ] _____
- [ ] _____
- [ ] _____

This or that: TV or movie? Chair or table? Arcade or movie theatre? Old or young? Chair or couch? Motel or hotel? Sitting or standing? Purple or Blue?

Date: ___ / ___ / ___

Day of the Week

S M T W TH F S

AM
PM

Today's Bitchin' Bestie!

(Name of person, pet, or thing)

Bitch Win of the Day

_____

_____

_____

_____

THE NUMBER OF FUCKS I DON'T GIVE TODAY

I'm fucking thankful for:

Create a Masterpiece

(or just scribble)

Bitch-sational Ramblings!

Shit to do

- [ ] _____
- [ ] _____
- [ ] _____
- [ ] _____
- [ ] _____
- [ ] _____
- [ ] _____
- [ ] _____

Random Crappery
Word of the day...

THOUGHT OF THE DAY:

This or that: Dishes or laundry? Fishing or hunting? Indie or classic rock? Pictures or videos? Black or white? Roses or sunflowers? New clothes or vintage?

Date: ___ / ___ / ___

Day of the Week

S M T W TH F S

AM
PM

My Bitch in Crime!

(Name of person, pet, or thing)

Bitchin' Thing That Happened

_____

_____

_____

_____

_____

THE NUMBER OF FUCKS I DON'T GIVE TODAY

I'm fucking thankful for:

OMG-ossip!

More Bitch-tacular Writings!

_____

_____

_____

_____

_____

_____

_____

Shit to do

- [ ] _____
- [ ] _____
- [ ] _____
- [ ] _____
- [ ] _____
- [ ] _____
- [ ] _____
- [ ] _____

Random Crappery

These [_____] make me [_____] .

This or that: Coffee or tea? Planet or star? Classical or techno? Cardio or strength? Detailed or abstract? Single or relationship? Kitten or puppy?

Date: ___ / ___ / ___

This Bitch Made My Day!

(Name of person, pet, or thing)

Today's Bitchin' Highlight

_____

_____

_____

_____

_____

THE NUMBER OF FUCKS I DON'T GIVE TODAY

I'm fucking thankful for:

Shopping Wish List:

Other Bitch-tastic Happenings!

_____
_____
_____
_____
_____
_____
_____
_____

Shit to do

- ☐ _____
- ☐ _____
- ☐ _____
- ☐ _____
- ☐ _____
- ☐ _____
- ☐ _____
- ☐ _____

Random Crappery
Color of the day...

" QUOTE OF THE DAY:

"

This or that: Soy milk or almond milk? Roller skating or ice skating? Solar system or Galaxy? Red or blue? Curly or straight? Cookies or cake?

Printed in Great Britain
by Amazon